How to use Fold-out Bikes

First, find the numbers from 1 to 50 on the sticker sheets and put them on the wall chart. Then add the bike stickers to the chart in your favourite order. You can peel them off again whenever you like, and put them back in a different order. On the back of the wall chart is a huge poster, and there are also seven mini posters of exciting bikes to pull out!

50 bike stickers to place on the chart in your favourite order

D1826976

Numbers to stick on the wall chart from 1 up to 50

My Top 50 Bikes

Add all the stickers to the wall chart in whatever order you like, from 1 to 50, and you can move them around if you change your mind!

Yamaha YZF-R1

On the back of the wall chart is a huge poster of this amazing bike!

Kawasaki

Ducatti ST4s

Suzuki RM85

Triumph D

Honda CB1000RR

Suzuki GSX-R600

7 mini posters to pull out and keep

Kawasaki Ninja ZX-6R

Yamaha V Star Classic

Suzuki RM85

Yamaha Warrior

Lehman Trikes Renegade

Triumph Scrambler

Suzuki GSX-R1000

Yamaha XT660X

Suzuki Burgman 650

Honda Silverwing

Honda Goldwing

Harley Davidson XL1200R

1	2	3	4	5	6	7	8
13	14	15	16	17	18	19	20
25	26	27	28	29	30	31	32
38	39	40	41	42	43	44	45

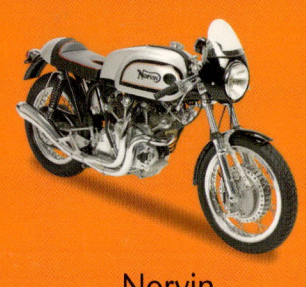

Norvin

1985 Suzuki GSX-R 750

Buell Ulysses

MZ 1000 S

2004 Suzuki GSX-R 750

BMW F650CS

Harley Davidson Nightster

Kawasaki Mean Streak

Egli Vincent

Royal Enfield Electra Jubilee

Kawasaki W650

BMW K1200 LT

Yamaha XVS1300A

Yamaha YZF-R1

Kawasaki Z1000

Suzuki Intruder M1800R

Yamaha XJR1300

Ducati 1000DS

Moto Guzzi MSG01

Honda XV1000 Varadero

Cagiva Raptor 1000

Kawasaki ZX10-R

BMW Megamoto HP2

Buell Lightning

2007 Suzuki GSX-R 750

Triumph Rocket Classic

Honda Zoomer

Harley Davidson UltraGlide

Buell 1125R

Suzuki DR125SM

Triumph Daytona

Suzuki VanVan

Suzuki Hayabusa

Suzuki Bandit 1250

BMW R1200C

Suzuki B King

Kawasaki ZZR1200

Harley Davidson FatBoy

Suzuki GSX-R1000

BMW R1150GS Adventure

Yamaha FZ1000S Fazer

9	10	11	12	
21	22	23	24	
33	34	35	36	37
46	47	48	49	50

Ducati ST4s

Triumph Daytona 675

Honda CB1000RR

Suzuki GSX-R600